My Family
Poems and Poetry From The Heart

The Way We Were

■**Cozzen Publications**
Claremont, North Carolina

Anna Huffman & Family

Copyright © 2007 Anna Huffman
All Rights Reserved

No part of this book may be reproduced, scanned, stored in a retrieval system, or transmitted and distributed in any printed or electronic form, by any means, without the written permission of the author.

This is a book of fiction. Names, characters, places, and incidents either are the product of the authors imagination or are used fictitiously, and any resemblance to actual persons, living or dead, business establishments, events, or locales is entirely coincidental.

ISBN 978-0-6151-7136-4

Printed in United States of America
Published by Cozzen Publications
First Edition

Anna Huffman & Family

My Family
Poems and Poetry From The Heart

The Way We Were

By Anna Huffman & Family

Anna Huffman & Family

In Memory of

Mother (Bernice Mongro)

Father (Kenneth Killian)

Brother (Gerold Killian)

Anna Huffman & Family

Contents

Introduction......13
Sommer Nichole Clark (Age 12)......15
      Never Knew......7
      Dragons......18
      Relationships......19
      I Miss you.......20
Kathlem Crane & Michael R. Holdren.......21
(Kathlem Crane)
      As We Search For Answers......23
      The End Is Near......24
      As The Night Goes On......25
(Michael R. Holdren)
      Life......26
      Seeing......27
      Lonely......28
Anna Huffman...31
      Flowers......33
      Can't Erase The Time......34
      Dear Loved Ones......36
      Don't Wait......37
      Doctors Overhaul......38
      December......39
      Alone,No.......40
      When We Are Old......41
      Lying Here......42
      Jump & Run......43
      I Am Complete.......44

To Fear.......45
Be Myself......46
Forgive.......47
To Serve......48
Always Loved.......49
To Mother, Family and Mikie......50
Aunt Minnie.......51
My Friend Vicke......52
Wish......53
Bay......54
Angel......55
Loves Me......56
The Cross......57
A Walk......58
Fear......59
Spring Time......60
Vale......61
Summer......62
The House......63
I Know The Sounds Of Animals......64
When He Gets Out Of Bed.......65
Pig Again......66
Lord God......67
God Knows.......68
My Love......69
Sweet Love......70
Death Is Before Me......71
God Made......72
Beginning......73
Sleep......74

Walked......75

Created......76

Day Will Bring......77

I Try......78

Be Nice......79

Boozing Mable......80

Because We Care......81

A Rose For Mother......82

Faded Quilt......83

My Favorite Quilt......85

My Stepfather, Danny......87

Mother-In-Law......88

Father-In-Law......89

Douglas Killian (Age 9)......91

Walking Alone......93

My Dog......94

My Grandpa.......95

My Girlfriend......96

Gerold Kenneth Killian......97

Daddy......99

The Letter......100

Judy Killian......101

Remember Me! *(For Family and Friends)*......103

Kim Killian......107

My Daddy......109

My Family Is Complete......111

What Went Wrong......112

Mothers......113

Robin Gale Killian......115

Haunted Lover......117

Sweet Revenge......118

Roger Killian......119

Me, My Daddy and Grandpa......121

Shelia Killian......123

Lost......125

Bernice Mongro......127

Man Power......129

Hurtful Words......130

All Blood Of The Same......131

Begin Manhood......133

Boy To Man......135

Ruth Oldham......137

When Tomorrow Starts Without Me......139

To Whom It Concerns......141

Danyell Robinette......143

Us......145

Hope......146

"Risk" (anonymous)......147

"Christmas In Heaven" (unknown)......148

Introduction

In the following pages you'll find writings by members of Anna Huffman's family, the youngest 8 years old.

This is a very close-knit family that has a unique way of expressing themselves on paper.

Each family member has submitted their writings for this book through Anna, who came up with the original concept for the book. Anna has spent numerous hours in her attempt to gather these unique writings from her family.

Anna comes from a family of 13, including her mother and father, 4 boys and 7 girls.

As the publisher I have found this to be an extraordinary compilation of poems, poetry and writings that capture the interest of the reader. You'll delve into the lives of this very exceptional family.

During my relationship with Anna, I'll feel I know each member personally through these writings. I hope you'll find them as interesting as I have.

R. Duane Cozzen
Cozzen Publications

Anna Huffman & Family

Sommer Nicole Clark
(Niece)

<u>Sommer Clark</u> *is 12 years old and was born in Catawba County.*
She like swimming and talking on the phone with her friends.

Anna Huffman & Family

Never Knew

I never knew my mom's side of the family,
Not even her.
When I was twelve-years-old I met my mom and my brother,
I even talked to my older sister.
I love all of them.

Even though they may get on my nerves,
I will always love them,
No matter what.

I will always love my other side of my family too.
Mostly my grandma for loving me the way she does,
And my other grandma too.

Most of all, I love my mama and daddy.

Dragons

Dragons are fierce,
But we make our mask dear.
We might have only been here a year,
But it's time to fly away,
Like all dragons do in their lives.

Anna Huffman & Family

Relationships

Relationships are all about trust.
    You should not tell a lie to the other person.
When you do you might end up all alone.
    If you think about cheating on a person,
You need to think of the other persons feelings,
    And how it would feel to be in there shoes.
So you should always be thinking of the other person that you are with.
    If you don't think you belong together then you need to talk about the problem to the other person.
Do not breakup with them, then and there.
    Not even if you want to.

I Miss You

I miss you being there with me, all the time,

When you and me would talk or just sit there together.

It would always make me feel a lot better.

I miss you saying good night and I love you.

And you always told me not to worry about you because God would take care of you.

But he just took you from me and I don't like that,

But I know you are in a better place where you don't hurt anymore,

But I will always miss you,

And you will always be in my heart.

In memory of Janet Sue Isenhour Clark

Anna Huffman & Family

Kathlem Crane & Michael R. Holden
(Niece & fiancée)

<u>Kathlem Crane</u> is 19 years old and was born in Mercer County, West Virginia.

She likes listening to country music and playing video games and working on the computer.

<u>Michael Holden</u> is 27 years old and was born in Mercer County, West Virginia.

He works as an electrician and is a very hard worker.

He likes working on cars, playing golf and video games.

He and Kathlem are engaged to be married.

Anna Huffman & Family

AS WE SEARCH FOR ANSWERS

AS THE CLOUDS GO DARKER,
THE NIGHT GETS COLDER.

HOW THE WEATHER IS CHANGING IN THE SEASONS.
HOW WE ARE GETTING OLDER.

HOW THE WORLD IS BECOMING,
WONDERING WHY SO MANY LOVE ONES ARE LOST.

THINKING THAT THE DAYS OF OUR LIVES ARE
GETTING SHORTER.

LOOKING FOR THE GRASS TO GET GREENER.
WANTING THE STARS TO GET BRIGHTER.

WONDERING IF FAMILY'S ARE GOING TO BE TOGETHER.
WANTING PLANTS AND LIFE TO GROW.

SEARCHING FOR HOPE AND WANTING TO FIND FAITH
IN THE LORD AND IN LIFE.

Kathlem Crane

My Family-Poems & Poetry From The Heart-The Way We Were

The End Is Near

Days go back.
Time, fading a lot.
I see my future,
I see my past.
I see what I have done, and what I want to do here.
I know I don't have much time here so I need to do what I'm here for.
Friends are slipping away and turning back.
Family's have become enemies.
Clouds are passing,
Stars are brighter.
The land and the mountains,
We cut and ruin.
Wars have begun, but in the end, they will vanish.
We don't see people for who they are,
We judge them by there appearance.
We know not to judge,
Because we can't.
But I say, in the end,
We will be judged by the Man up above.
So my advice to you is,
Watch what you do and say,
Especially how you got by doing it.

Kathlem Crane

Anna Huffman & Family

As The Night Goes On

We may fight and argue.

But as the night goes on,

We seem to find ourselves loving each other more and more.

He watches his sleeping beauty, while she dreams of him throughout the night.

She watches him work throughout the day, knowing he is the one.

Eyes may judge them, but they know what they want.

He is stronger then she, but she has that special gift, just for him.

She watches him sleep peacefully throughout the night, and wonders why he loves her.

She looks into his eyes, and then knows why.

He and she are two people, soon to be one.

As he holds her throughout the night, she knows how much he loves her.

As she says goodnight, she is at peace.

As he says I Love You, he knows she will always be there by his side.

Dedicated to my Love;

Michael Holdren

Kathlem Crane

My Family-Poems & Poetry From The Heart-The Way We Were

Life

With a smile that lifts the spirit of a soul.
A voice that lifts mind from a hole.
Eyes so bright they can light up the night.
    A laugh that brings smiles to another life.

Hands that have the touch of softness so rife.
Warmth in the arms that can remove the hearts bugs.
Kisses so lovely they make you forget about the worlds tugs.
    A mind so strong and a heart that cares.

Words of wisdom, helps mend the unfriendly tears.
Friendship to give and feeling to share.
Ears that listen to others, whose lives are treated unfair.
    Beauty that's there, for ones eyes to see.

With curves so sleek and the power to set one free.
To have a heart of gold, priceless as it may be.
Fragile and tender, never to stray nor flee.
To share the same dream that's special to me.

    Dedicated to a special lady.
    Promise you'll never be shady.

Michael R. Holdren

Anna Huffman & Family

Seeing

Along the road of traveled souls,
Comes a time for life to unfold.
Like a hawk flying through the sky,
With his eyes keen and bold.
    The flowers, how their blooms are full of color,
    And makes eyes bright.
    There's nothing to be worried about,
    As long as your prays are said at night.
With a smile on our face,
You'll lift another's weary spirit, thats a goal..
Now with obstacle's that shall block your way,
Fight back and pay the toll.
    Another fork in the tree,
    You will come to hold on tight to prevent the fall.
    With a brain and heart,
    Anything can be achieved, after breaking the wall.
Like a salmon swimming upstream,
The journey is very rough.
Once you have made it to that spot,
It doesn't seem so tough.
    With a heavy shoulder,
    The weight can always be dealt with.
    Just remember, in the words of wisdom,
    Sometimes its best to plead the fifth.

                                              Michael R. Holdren

Lonely

◆

All mixed up in the ramble of the heavy heart,

Reached out to lend a hand,

To help others get a start.

Left out of a picture that never really existed.

To be used and abused, and everything is black listed.

Having a feeling that just can't be revealing.

Wishing for a relief in the turn of a cheek, to be sealing.

An open wound looking for the stitches and bandages.

Grown to be somewhat wiser throughout the ages.

With each good deed done, still standing last in line.

Where is the moral support?

Somebody tell me everything is fine.

Greasy hands and well oiled pride.

Worked for my piece of the pie.

Thought of the values of life,

To fool the pesky sky.

Downhearted now,

Looking for the road to success.

Finding where to start,

Where it begins to recess.

Whatever may fall from the start,

Is God's will.

Standing strong and still,

Voicing opinion at will.

Anna Huffman & Family

Nevertheless, when will the tide go back to the sea.
When will the time come for troubles to flee.
No matter how nice you can be,
Some are still mean.
Heaven-bound,
So keep the burdened soul clean.
No love can be lost,
If no love is found.
So here we go again,
Starting from the ground.
For once I would like to give her the KO,
In the round

Michael R. Holdren

Anna Huffman & Family

Anna Huffman

Anna Huffman was born and raised in Catawba County, North Carolina and has been married for over 26 years.

Anna believes in forgiveness and Jesus Christ, who died for our sins.

Besides reading poems and poetry, her favorite book is the Holy Bible.

Anna Huffman & Family

Flowers

As I sit and look at the yellow flowers,
I think of all the things we went through.

And all the things we *will* be going through,
    Because you care,
        Always my love,
            My only one.

As I sit and see the yellow flowers,
I think of you and our love for one another.

                                      Anna Huffman

Can't Erase Time

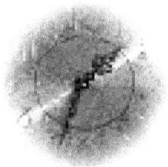

There are levels to climb each day.
Does it matter what anyone might say?
As long as you are right in climbing each step.
You want have a second chance after you have stepped!
Time will not go backwards, for even one minute.
Go on forward.
Watch your mistakes,
There might be plenty.
Never hurt another on each step you stand.
The hurt will always carry on as though it were sand.
Mend a broken heart that's caused by you.
Try to erase that hurt and make anew,
The love and closeness that was once shared,
Least it grows to separate the love that was once a pair.
Can't you find a way to make it right?
Before it's brought into the light.
Those unkind words will never be forgotten,
They only fade in time.
That scale upon the heart will always be there,

Anna Huffman & Family

To come and go as a swamp of slime.

Be careful of each one you push away.

He or she could be the one to hold you up one day.

Our deeds are recorded in heaven's Holy Book,

That we might be judged down each pathway and nook.

You can hold up your head with power and dignity,

But the day will pass when we come,

Face to face with eternity.

Anna Huffman

Dear Loved Ones

God saw him growing weary,
So God did what he thought was best.
He came and stood beside him,
And whispered come and rest.

  He bade none a last farewell,
  Not even said goodbye.
  He was gone before we he knew it
  And only God knows why.

A million times we have needed him.
A million times we have cried.
If love alone could have saved him,
He never would have died.

  In life we loved him dearly.
  In death we love him still.
  In our hearts he holds a place,
  No one can ever fill.

It broke our hearts to lose him.
But he didn't go alone.
For part of us went with him.
The day God called him home.

Anna Huffman

Anna Huffman & Family

Don't Wait

Don't wait for me baby.
I won't be around for you to see.
I'll just drift on down the highway,
That will take me away from you.

I'll remember all the good times.
Each night I lay down to sleep,
I'll think of all the love we shared,
And all the promises I never meant to keep.

I have broken you heart, I know.
But not near as much as I feel now.
There's no turning back on this lonely road.
I must travel these old roads as far as they will go.

I'll dream of you many times, I know.
But I'll never get to close to show.
Don't waste you years on me, baby.
I can never say I love you – only maybe.

Anna Huffman

Doctors Overhaul

Oh our doctors of so many faces.
      They can stop the blood that flows.
They can sew and patch you head to toe.
      Make you feel good when you're low.
They can even change our parts,
      Hips, kidneys and hearts.
Doctors can replace your bones with plastic,
      Even your veins and teeth, like magic.
Yeah, and when that heart goes on the blink,
      You will stop and think,
Before the Angels can call your life final.
      How proud you are when recovery is made new.
I have made it when others are but few.
      Even though you know your years are but a few.
And your overhaul want last.
      One day, you will too, go on beyond the blue.

Anna Huffman & Family

DECEMBER

Full moon in a clear December sky.
With it so cold,
We hold each other close.

Our noses are so cold,
But our lips are so warm,
When we kiss.

Under the shiny stars,
We hold on to each other,
As the wind blows so cold.

We keep each other warm,
Under the December sky.

Anna Huffman

Alone, No

You say you walk alone.
But you are not.
God is with you,
And so am I.

If you say you walk alone,
And I am not there,
You are still not alone.
God is always there.

You are sweet and gentle,
Because God is with you,
All the time.

Anna Huffman

When We Are Old

One night, when we are old and the moon is full,
We will be sitting own the porch swing,
Looking at the sky.

When we are old,
We still hold each other.

When we are old,
We will kiss each other on the head.

When we are old,
We know this night is all ours,
With peace around us.

When we are old.

Anna Huffman

Lying Here

Lying here beside you,
My cheek against yours,
And yours against mine.
We will think of all the good times,
And try to forget the bad,
For we are one.
Our hearts beat slow as one,
For we are one.
When we are together,
Lying here beside each other.

Anna Huffman

Anna Huffman & Family

JUMP and RUN

✶✶✶✶✶✶✶

JUMP LIKE A BUNNY,
MOVE LIKE A TREE.
COME ON HONEY,
COME WITH ME

MOVE LIKE A RAT,
RUN LIKE A DOG
COME ON WITH ME.

JUMP UP, HIT YOUR HEAD,
COME, LET'S GO OVER THE HILL.

LET'S GO THIS WAY AND THAT WAY,
AND RUN ALL AROUND.

Anna Huffman

(44)
I Am Complete
✞✞✞✞✞✞✞✞✞✞✞

Christ is alive in my heart.

God is at work in my live.

I am becoming what he created me to be.

I have love, joy, peace, kindness, goodness and faith.

He fills all the empty places in my heart.

I am complete, because I know Him.

ARE YOU COMPLETE?

Anna Huffman

Anna Huffman & Family

TO FEAR

YOU CAN FEAR ANYTHING.
LIKE MONSTERS UNDER THE BED.
A BUMP IN THE NIGHT.
BEING ALONE IN THE DARK AT NIGHT.
LOUD THUNDERSTORMS THAT YOU ARE AFRAID OF.

BUT

Daddy was always there,

And Mom to calm you down.

And all the time,

We have had our heavenly Father,

Who quiets our fears.

Anna Huffman

Be Myself

I can be myself.
I can make people happy.
I am romantic.
I am sad.
I am happy.
I can cry.
I can enjoy life or anything life brings my way.
I can talk on the phone.
I don't like housework.
I like to write.
I love and spoil my pets,
But most of all,
I have a passion for studying God's word.

Anna Huffman

Forgive

If any one hurts me,
Or I hurt them.

    I can say,
      Sorry, I forgive you.

If they hurt me,
I still can forgive them.
'Cause in God's eyes,
That's what you do.

    So I can forgive.

I will always forgive others!

                                       Anna Huffman

To Serve

✞✞✞✞✞

I TRY TO DO MY BEST,
    TO SERVE.

I CHOOSE TO *SERVE*,
I DO ALL THAT I CAN.

I DO EVERYTHING THAT I CAN,
    TO SERVE.

BUT THERE IS ONLY ONE,
    I WILL *SERVE* THE MOST.

AND THAT IS THE LORD!

    AND I WILL ALWAYS,
TRY TO *SERVE HIM.*

Anna Huffman

Always Loved

    I am always loved.
No matter how alone I am.

If I never have friends or family in my life,
    I am always loved.

If I never have a man to hold me,
    I will always be loved.

Because God loves me,
And I love him.

    That's why I am always loved.

Anna Huffman

(50)
To Mother, Family and Mikie
☐☐☐☐☐☐☐☐☐☐☐☐☐☐

I am not far a way,
I am in your hearts.
So just remember,
I love you all.
Don't cry or be sad,
I am with God,
And it's beautiful up here.
So don't cry my dear ones.
Wipe away the tears.
You will see me again someday,
And we will be together forever with God.

To the Dill Family and Husband
2/23/2003
We will miss her very much and we are thinking of you all.
God Bless!

Anna Huffman

Anna Huffman & Family

(51)
Aunt Minnie

I will miss you very much

But I know you are not far away

You are in my heart

Your are with God now in a peaceful place now with no pain

I will always love you and I will see you again someday and we will be

together again

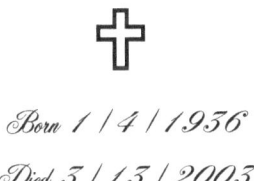

Born 1/4/1936
Died 3/13/2003

Anna Huffman

My Family-Poems & Poetry From The Heart-The Way We Were

(52)
MY FRIEND VICKE
● ● ● ● ● ● ●

SHE IS MY FRIEND.

●

I CAN TALK TO HER AND TELL HER HOW I FEEL INSIDE.

●

I CAN TELL HER ANYTHING.

●

SHE IS A GOOD FRIEND THAT WANT LET ME DOWN.

●

SHE IS A FRIEND AND MEANS A WHOLE LOT TO ME.

●

SHE IS MY NEICE.

●

AND I LOVE HER.

●

THAT'S WHAT FRIENDS ARE FOR.

●

TO NEVER TELL

Anna Huffman

Wish

Wish I may
Wish I might
For all our dreams will come true

Wish I may
Wish I see
That everything will come out right

Wish I knew you loved me so
Oh how I wish I knew
But most of all I wish and know
God loves us both so

Anna Huffman

Bay

I had a dog I called Bay.
I had him for a very long time.
He was eighteen-years-old.
One day we came home and he could not walk.
He was in pain.
It hurt me to see him that way.
The next day he still could not walk.
He was still in pain.
We had to have him put to sleep.
Then I cried because I lost my dog named Bay.
I miss him very much.
Some day's I look for him,
But he is gone to a better place.
He was like my child that I lost.
My boy Bay.

Anna Huffman

ANGEL

SOME PEOPLE SAY
WE COME BACK AS SOMETHING ELSE.
I WANT TO COME BACK AS AN ANGEL,
TO WATCH OVER PEOPLE.
TO BE WITH THEM EVER STEP OF THE WAY.
GIVE THEM COMFORT,
WHEN BAD TIMES ARE AROUND,
AND GOOD ONES TOO.
TO LOOK OVER THE CHILDREN,
AND MANY MORE.
I CAN FLY HIGH UP IN THE SKY,
AND HELP GOD WHEN HE NEEDS ME.

Anna Huffman

Loves Me

Jesus loves me,
Yes I know.

Now I need to know if you love me,
Like Jesus does.

'Cause I love you,
Like Jesus loves me.

But most of all,
I love Jesus too,
As much as He loves me.

Now you know,
Just how I feel.

Anna Huffman

Anna Huffman & Family

The Cross

Because of the **Cross**,
The world is forever changed,
And all of **God's** blessings are now yours.

Because of the **Cross**,
You have been forgiven.
A life filled with **love, joy, strength and freedom.**
Freedom from fear and anxiety from the storms of life, and so much more.

Because of the Cross,
You will never be the same.

Anna Huffman

A Walk

When I walk through the mowed yard,

A heavy dew clings to the side of my feet.

It's fun to be out to see the stars.

The night is warm, the moon is blue.

I can't wait until you come home soon.

Anna Huffman

(59)
Fear

When the wind works against us in the dark,
It fills us full of fear.
We count on our strength,
Like a child in the night.
How the cold creeps around us,
When the fire goes out.
Our hearts beat as one,
Until we go in,
To save ourselves.

Anna Huffman

Spring Time

Oh, give us pleasure in the flower today.
Give us not to think so far away.

Keep us here in the simple springtime of the year.
Give us the pleasure of the white rose,
Make us happy as the day goes,
As we hold hands and walk down the path of the pretty white rose.

With these pretty blossoms,
I reach out to kiss you,
In the springtime of the year.
A pretty bed of white roses,
For me and you.

Anna Huffman

Vale

When I was young,
I went to see the vale.

    This vale was like it was holding me so close,
    I felt warm inside.

The vale was quiet, but sweet,
As the wind blew.

    That night with a mist,
    That was sweet, you see.

I could not leave this vale,
Because I love this vale.

    The first time I saw it,
    It was the vale for me.
    Always in my dreams.

Look up Dale,
Because Dales means vale.
He is mine.

                                    Anna Huffman

Summer

TODAY IS A PRETTY DAY,
WITH BLUE SKY, GREE TREES AND NOT SO HOT.

IT WILL BE A GREAT DAY,
FOR THIS IS THE FIRST DAY OF SUMMER.

SUMMER IS NICE TODAY,
NOT AS HOT FOR SUMMER TO BE HERE.

TODAY IS SUMMER,
THE VERY FIRST DAY

Anna Huffman

The House

Household of thirteen.

Beds of five.

When it gets late,

What can we do?

Bed for four.

Bed for three.

Bed for two.

Bed for two,

And a bed for two more.

A bed for mother and father.

We all went to sleep in these little beds and rooms.

That's the life I new,

When I was small.

Like the little old woman in the shoe.

Anna Huffman

I Know The Sounds Of Animals

I know the sounds of animals.
When he walks up,
He roars like a mouse.
He purrs like a mouse.
He hoots like a duck,
And moos like a goose

He squeaks like a cat.
He quacks like a dog.
He oinks like a bear,
And a big one at that.

He honks like a hog.
He croaks like a cow.
He barks like a bee.

No wonder I know the sounds of him.

Anna Huffman

Anna Huffman & Family

When He Gets Out Of Bed

As soon as he gets up out of the bed,
His underwear goes on his head.

I laugh at him and tell him,
Don't put them there own your head,
'Cause there's no place for his underwear but near his ears.

Above his brain,
Where his underwear remains,
Why want anyone tell him,
They go on his toes.

Anna Huffman

Pigs Again
〇〇〇〇

You're eating like a pig again.
If you keep eating like a pig,
You'll become one!

And he said to me, "Don't I have a lovely tail?"

Anna Huffman

LORD GOD

THE LORD GOD SAID THERE IS A MAN ON EARTH BELOW, WHOM I WOULD HELP HIS SOUL.

THE MASTER OF DREAMS, THE LORD GOD SAID, YOU MUST SHOW MY DIVINE LOVE FOR HIM.

I FEAR THAT IF YOU DON'T,
IT WILL BE TOO LATE.

Anna Huffman

God Knows

✞✞✞✞✞✞✞✞✞✞

A Man, God knows, came for me.
The Good Spirit knew,
But He would not tell.
> There are things you should not know.

The Man will come for you,
But we will never know.
> Only God knows when He will come for you.

Anna Huffman

My Love

I see you, my love
From the hills upon the mountains.

Now as I walk to the window,
I see you, my love

You call out to me,
And say, come my love.
Come away with me.

With the birds, trees and sky so blue,
I went way, with you.

Anna Huffman

(70)
Sweet Love

You are mine, my love.

My heart hurts to reach out to the heights of your love.

See sweetheart, when we sit and hold hands.

See the birds and trees as we sing.

We go out into the fields and lay there looking at the sky.

For you are mine,

As the clouds go by.

Anna Huffman

Anna Huffman & Family

Death Is Before Me

Death is before me today.
Like health to the sick.
Like leaving the bedroom,
After sickness.

Death is before me today.
Like sitting under a cloth,
On a day of wind.

Death is before me today.
Like sitting down on the shore of drunkenness.

Death is before me today.
Like the end of a rain storm.

Death is before me today.
Like the sky when it clears,
After it rains.

    When the war is over.

Anna Huffman

God Made

WHEN GOD MADE LITTLE GIRLS,
HE MADE THEM SWEET AS PIE,
TO TAKE CARE OF EACH OTHER,
AS THEY GO BY.

WHEN GOD MADE LITTLE BOYS,
HE MADE THEM NICE AND STRONG,
TO TAKE CARE OF EACH OTHER,
AS THEY GO BY.

Anna Huffman

Beginning

When we go down the road of life,
When peace and joy comes across us.
Remember the good times we had.
For we forget what life is all about.
But each day will get better along the way.
As we walk down the road,
God is with us every stop of the way.

Anna Huffman

Sleep

I went to sleep that night.
    Everything seemed alright.
When I awoke,
    You were gone.
And I don't know why I was alone.
    As I sit, I think.
I'm not alone!
    God is with me,
I will never be alone.
    For i have Thee with me,
All the time.

Anna Huffman

Walked

We've walked so far together.
We've grown so very close,
But now our life has changed,
And we don't know where to go from here.
I want to see what you want in life.
As for me, all I want is you and God in my life.

                                                Anna Huffman

Created

I do believe that God above created you and me to love.
He sent you down from all the rest,
Because He knows I love you best.
I do love you best.

    Most of all, I love God,
    For giving me you to love.

Anna Huffman

Day Will Bring

As I sit on the swing with my little dog, listening to the birds sing, I wonder what the day will bring and how it will go.

Then I went into the house to eat and feed my little dog.

I began to clean.

Then I sat down and began to write some poems.

Now I know how my day went.

As I sit and think of God and how He made my day a good one today.

Anna Huffman

I Try

I tell the truth.
I try my best.
I try with all my heart,
But nothing seems to help.
    Every time I try,
    Everything goes wrong,
    So I give up,
    And not try so hard.
Maybe something will come out right,
But I know I am not alone.
God is with me all along,
So I an never alone.

Anna Huffman

Be Nice

I hurt people,
I made them sad,
I made them mad.
In God's name I take it all back.
It is what you should do.
You forgave me,
But first You say I must tell them I am sorry.
Tell them you love them and will never do it again.
God as my witness,
I will be nice and true to all I see and meet along the way.
I will be nice,
For that is what everyone should do.

Anna Huffman

(80)
Boozing Mable

As I sit at the dinning room table,
Thinking of things to do,
I hear old Mable.
The cantankerous old lady who lives over the hill.
She loves to pass by mocking the whippoorwill.

She can't fool me, I know where she lives.
She is carrying a bottle and passed by for a lend.
The liquor still that's been running for years.
Mable knows where to go through the fields.

By the time she starts back this way,
She has picked up speed and has nothing to say.
As she goes down the hill, past the creek,
She looks so lively and yet so very meek.

But soon you can hear her cussing her man.
She gets so rowdy slinging that frying pan.
Poor old man doesn't have a chance to his hand.
She cracks his knuckles and he lands her in the sand.

We don't need TV, we have a good show that will last,
For a few hours of mud slinging, from the past.
When Mabel's booze is getting low in her shiny flask,
PA is getting ready to run,
Bet, real fast.

Anna Huffman & Family

Because We Care

We begin a new year.

Hopeful for those we love, so dear.

For friends and loved ones who have come from far and near,

To be there, if any is in despair.

It's a happy day, because we care.

Some of us are getting old and turning gray.

But there's a new beginning every day.

Our lives will guide a child someday.

Loving, caring and walk the same path another day.

It's a happy day, because we care.

Anna Huffman

A Rose For Mother

We have set aside each year, just one day.
So our loving memories will not fade.
This special day is for my special friend, my mother,
Who loved and cherished me above all other.
She was the rock I depended on, to hold me close,
When things went wrong.
My mother was a special friend.
A sweet voice in every song.
I can still see and hear, the laughter, teardrops, pleasure and pain.
As I stroll down this pathway of triumphs, defeats, losses and gains.
One day, I too must leave this world with all its dreams.
I have climbed my mountain, searched and found my scene.
While I live upon this plain,
Days, weeks and months go by.
I will always honor the loving memory of my dear mother.
My dear mother, who has gone on above the sky.

Anna Huffman

Anna Huffman & Family

Faded Quilt

I can still see my mother as she sewed,

    The quilt she made for me.

With all its many colors, as if she knew,

    This quilt would be treasured beyond the blue.

This quilt has covered many through the years.

    To comfort a baby or mother with tears.

Its warmth for many nights of peaceful love.

    Its many colors, so soft, of the pattern of a dove.

This old quilt brought peace and happiness to so many.

    On cold, cold nights, it brought warmth a plenty.

Its been handed down from one generation to another.

    I wonder is she is looking on, my dear mother.

You worked so hard to put the pieces together just right.

    How you would pedal that machine up into the night.

And how hard you worked with your feet,

    Just to make this beautiful quilt so neat.

As I put this quilt on its shelf for another to use,

    I know it can't stand many more years of abuse.

This quilt was made for me to treasure.

    The love of this faded quilt is without measure.

If you should be looking down from above,

You'll see I am sewing a quilt to pass on with love.
I hope my labor won't be in vain.
It's hoped they will remember me also, without pain.
I will make each stitch with you in mind.
This beautiful quilt that's yours, ours, and mine.

Anna Huffman

My Favorite Quilt

I have memories of my dear old mother,

As she worked into the night,

For my brother and I,

A satin quilt of many colors she did make,

To leave for us as a keepsake.

To keep us warm on a cold winters night.

Many years have come and gone

Since the colors of that old quilt have shined so bright.

But in my mind and heart,

Those colors will never fade.

They will sparkle and shine,

No matter where its laid.

This quilt has been a comfort for kids when sick.

A comfort when there's a problem to be fixed.

When there's a need for tender loving care.

Such a comfort to wrap up in and see its flair.

Its weathered many a cold night with its warmth,

Upon the old feathered bed, so very soft.

I think of all the pieces she put together,

And of each stitch she made.

She so tenderly selected pieces she knew would not fade.

My mother so kind and thoughtful and so dear.

I would trade it for fear I would loose my memories so dear.

Sound memories to pass down to my children,

And more memories it brings each day.

Thank you mother for all the sweet memories you left me.

Your memory will always be with me,

For me to cherish.

I'll leave behind the same,

So my children will not perish

Anna Huffman

My Stepfather, Danny

You will always be in my life.
You were always there when I needed you.
Now you need me,
And I will always be there.
If I am not there at times,
Just remember you are always in my heart and soul, forever.
I love you and you will always be my stepfather Danny.

Anna Huffman

Mother-In-Law

I have a mother-in-law.
She is as sweet as she can be.
She told me that she loved me,
And that made me feel good inside.
I did not feel alone.
I hope I never lose her,
Because I have no mother.
God keep her in a prayer,
So she will be with me,
So she will be around.
I can still have a mother, one more time,
For I have no family at this time, or a mother.
I love my mother-in-law.

Anna Huffman

Father-In-Law

△ △ △ △

I have a father-in-law,
    Who I care about so much.
I don't know why he likes me,
    But I will always love him so.
When I have no more fathers.
    He is all I have.
He is a sweet man.
    I hope I never lose him,
But maybe I have.
    God keep him safe and in a prayer to keep him around,
So I can have a father, one more time, and in my life,
    Because I lost the ones I had.

Anna Huffman

Anna Huffman & Family

Douglas Killian

Douglas is 9 years old and was born in Catawba County, North Carolina.

He likes swimming, roller skating and bowling.

He is also in the Cub Scouts.

Anna Huffman & Family

Walking Alone

You might think you are walking alone,

But you are not,

Because God is with you all the time.

So don't think you are walking alone, ever again.

You can not see God,

But He is always with you,

In winter,

In summer air,

In the fall leaves,

Even in the springs flowers.

Douglas Killian

My Dog

I had a dog name Midge,
When I was a baby.

He was a good dog.
But one day,
Midge got sick,
And passed away.

He is in a better place.

Douglas Killian

Anna Huffman & Family

My Grandpa

My grandpa was a truck driver
But he loved trains.
He was a very good man.
One night, he passed away.
After our family drove for hours and hours to get there,
It was over.
We were all sad to see him go,
But he's in a better place now.
We will always love
"Pop Dad".

In memory of Ron "Pop Dad" Oldham
Passed April 2, 2003

Douglas Killian

My Girlfriend

I will always be there for my girlfriend.
She will always be there for me.
I love her.
She loves me.
I will always be her boyfriend.
She will always be my girlfriend.
Nothing can break us up.
Nothing will break us up, ever.
I will always love her.

Douglas Killian

Anna Huffman & Family

Gerald Kenneth Killian

Loving brother.
Born 3-11-1949 - Died 4-30-91

    Gerald Kenneth Killian was the oldest child in the family. Though he stayed in trouble a lot, we loved him very much and miss him.

    He didn't want to live with anyone so he stayed homeless most of the time. Mom would always give him money and food, as did the rest of the family.

    Gerald was killed by a train in 1991.

    God rest his soul!

Anna Huffman & Family

Daddy

<u>You loved me enough;</u>
    To bug me about where I was going,
    With whom,
    And what time I would get home.
<u>You loved me enough;</u>
    To be silent,
    And let me discover my hand picked friend was a creep.
<u>You loved me enough;</u>
    To make me return a ring to a jewelry store,
    And confess I stole it.
<u>You loved me enough;</u>
    To ignore what every other father did.
<u>You loved me enough;</u>
    To let me stumble, fall and fail,
    So that I could learn to stand alone.
<u>You loved me enough;</u>
    To accept me for what I was,
    Not what you wanted me to be.

                                        Gerald Kenneth Killian
                                        Fathers Day 1988

The Letter

♦♦♦♦♦♦♦♦♦♦♦♦

To whom it may concern;

    I could have sought, by wit or will. You fight dream to dim; and yet, if I swayed you with a smile, my reward would be regret.

    Take my silence, tho intended. Take my courage now pretended.

    You my love, will make it real!

Gerald Kenneth Killian

Judy Killian

Judy Killian was born in Catawba County, North Carolina.

She is the oldest girl in the family.

She has only been married once and has a child and grand-child.

Judy now lives in Maryland where she loves spending her time making quilts.

Anna Huffman & Family

Remember Me

(For family and friends)

When I am gone,
> And no longer live,

Remember the love,
> That I did give.

Remember the days,
> Of good and bad.

Remember me,
> And don't be sad.

I've journeyed through,
> This earthly place.

Remember the smile,
> Upon my face.

Remember the name,
> You gave to me.

That's the one,
> I'll always be.

Remember the cake,
> With icing so pink.

Of all the tea,
> That we did drink.

Remember the steaks,
> Grilled in the rain.

The joy and laughter,
> Of people insane.

Remember the truth,
> Of Santa Claus.

Remember our trip,
> To the shopping malls.

Remember the times
> Of riding to see,

What the world held,
> As a mystery?

Remember the crafts,
> That we did make.

All made of love,
> With no mistakes.

Remember the nanny,
> Who love you so?

Watching with love,
> As you did grow.

Remember your mom,
> My precious son.

Remember all the good,
> That I had done.

Anna Huffman & Family

Remember the sewing,
> I tried to teach.

Keep on trying,
> Your goal to reach.

Remember the wife,
> And that special glance,

Who only wanted only,
> A second chance.

Yes, remember me,
> Through good and bad,

Forgive the worst,
> And please be glad.

I'll always love,
> How each changed by my life,

With prayers of love,
> Each and every night.

REMEMBER ME......................

Judy Killian

Anna Huffman & Family

Kim Killian

Kim Killian is 39-years-old and was born in Mansfield, Ohio but has lived in Catawba County for the past 15 years.

She likes swimming, bowling and reading.

Anna Huffman & Family

My Daddy
❖ ❖ ❖ ❖

Daddy was a good man.
Couldn't always count on him.

Sometimes he wasn't my biggest fan.
I was his oldest daughter Kim.

I got remarried and had a new life.
Not seeing Dad for a few years.

He had also taken a new wife.
Over the years my mind was turning gears.

Dad suddenly got sick.
We drove for several hours.

We had to get there really quick.
Had to do everything within my powers.

Was with him for several weeks,
When everything got much worse.

There weren't many good peaks.
It's like we were under a curse.

(110)

Daddy was already gone.
We were all in pain.

He passed away around dawn.
Nobody had anything to gain.

We still really miss him today.
All we do now is pray.

So much that we can't replay,
That's all I can say.

Kim Killian

Anna Huffman & Family

My Family Is Complete

I've always had a youngest son,
Since the day he was born.
My oldest daughter and I,
Have bee close for years now.
But just last week my middle daughter,
Came back to me.
No I feel whole again.
God finally brought all my children back to me.
And that's a good feeling.
That's why I say,
My family is complete now.
THANKS TO GOD!

Kim Killian

What Went Wrong?
? ? ? ? ? ? ? ? ?

We were once a family.
We had some happy times,
Along with sad times.
> *What went wrong?*

We went through a lot together.
The good and the bad.
When things got really bad,
I couldn't take it anymore.
> *What went wrong?*

Our family got torn apart,
Right before our eyes,
And that broke my heart.
> *What went wrong?*

Through all the years,
Your were all thought about.
Somethings can't be changed.
Somethings can.
Maybe now we can finally see,,
> *What went wrong!*

Kim Killian

Anna Huffman & Family

Mothers

Mothers are people too.
Especially when you're feeling blue.

They can cheer you up in a hurry.
Then things may not be so blurry.

Mothers are so very full of love.
They let you spread your wings like a dove.

They let us make our own choices, good or bad.
And sometimes we make them sad.

Mothers are here to stay, forever.
All we need to do is get along together.

They are special in every way.
We need to see that, everyday.

Mothers are here to stay.
So let's just pray.

Kim Killian

Anna Huffman & Family

Robin Gale Killian

I was born in Catawba County, North Carolina.

I am the fourth girl in the family.

I have three sons and two grand-children.

I've been married twice in my life and like doing crafts.

Anna Huffman & Family

Haunted Lover

I HAVE A POWER TO DRAW YOU NEAR.
MY VOICE YOU'LL ALWAYS HEAR.
MY EYES YOU'LL ALWAYS SEE,
BECAUSE I'LL NEVER LET YOU BE.

YOU'LL SEE ME IN YOUR DREAMS,
AND EVERYWHERE, IT WILL SEEM,
BECAUSE YOUR REGRET FOR LOSING ME,
HAS BEGUN TO HAUNT YOU, YOU SEE.

YOU WONDER WHY I DO THIS TO YOU,
AND WHY I LET YOU BE SO BLUE,
BECAUSE MY DEAREST, YOU BROKE MY HEART,
AND YOU'VE TORN OUR LOVE AND LIFE APART.

SWEET REVENGER

Robin Gale Killian

Sweet Revenge

I thought you loved me.
    But I found out that's not so.
I hope you will see,
    I have finally let you go.

We're not lovers, or even friends.
    Because our relation has come to end.
All day I think of you,
    And now you made me all so blue.

Someday you'll understand,
    Just why I picked you.
And how I had planned,
    For you too, to be blue.

Someday you'll come my way,
    And I'll be already gone.
Because now you will pay,
    For leaving me, all alone.

                              Sweet Revenger

                                    Robin Gale Killian

Anna Huffman & Family

Roger Killian

Roger Killian is 49 years old and was born in Catawba County, North Carolina.

He likes taking long naps and watching television.

Anna Huffman & Family

Me, My Daddy & Grandpa

I am old and white headed.
I look like my Daddy.
I walk like my Daddy.
I have things about me, like my Daddy.
But my temper is like my Grandpa.
And when it's like that,
You better watch out,
Because he was pretty mean when he got mad.

Roger Killian

Anna Huffman & Family

Sheila Killian

Two score and thirteen-years-ago, I was born in Newton, North Carolina. The fourth child, second daughter.

I like to read historical romance novels and taking trips to the beach.

I would like to write a book but I can't spell and the words wouldn't come out of the end of my pen anyway.

I have been married twice and have one child, three grandchildren and a great-grandchild, on the way.

I believe I should have been born in a different time and place.

Anna Huffman & Family

Lost

Lost, yesterday, somewhere,
Between sunrise and sunset.
Two golden hours,
Each set with sixty diamond minutes.
No reward is offered,
For they are now lost.
They are gone forever.

Sheila Killian

Anna Huffman & Family

Bernice Mongro

Bernice Mongro was raised in Catawba County, North Carolina and is the mother of 11 children.

She was married for 25 years, divorced and then remarried.

She has 30 grandchildren and lots of great-grandchildren.

Bernice was loved very much by her family and is missed.

She was a kind person that took care of anyone who needed help or caring.

She never let anyone go without food or anything else they may need.

She was a good mother.

Bernice died at the age of 65 in her sleep.

Anna Huffman & Family

Man Power

You can see me sitting so straight in my tower,
Thinking, boy I am somebody, I have power.
I can sit here doing nothing by the hour,
While you are behind this high fence, looking so sour.

If you get too close to the fence, dramatize.
My actions can be very quick before you realize.
Each waking hour is for me to push and criticize.
I have power over you until your time expires.

I'm thinking of all the things I have gotten by with.
I am no better than you are, if you get my drift.
As long as I am sitting over you, I'm in control.
Until you have finished your time, we own your soul.

I drink booze, gamble and run around on my wife.
I pull shady deals and am very careful with my life.
I like carrying the keys and locking the doors,
Know you can't walk out and go to the store.

I laugh within myself when I see you in pain,
Knowing very well how you listen each time you hear the train.
As you look so lonely looking out across the plains.
But you wouldn't dare to cross that fence of pain.

Bernice Mongro

My Family-Poems & Poetry From The Heart-The Way We Were

Hurtful Words

How can a son, or daughter, hurt a mother so bad?
In unkind words they throw like sand.
Children can break a mother's heart so bad.
Whey they speak those hateful words that makes her so sad.
Those words that come so quick,
Can hurt as if you were stabbed with a pick.
It will always leave a deep scar.
So hurtful at times you feel like a car struck you.
Time will erase the hurt somewhat,
But you can never erase the scar from the heart.
If can fade, as time goes on, for a while.
Just don't dwell on it, just pass on with a smile.
Find a place in your heart to love and forgive.
Just go on smiling and don't forget to live.
Watch those hurtful words, you speak so free.
Those hurtful words will blind you before you can see,
That the love they have for you is hard to deny,
From someone else that could never be so blind.
Don't be so cross,
Live one day at a time.
Love one another,
So you'll have a good peace of mind.

Bernice Mongro

All Blood Of The Same

There is always a place we call home.
Whether we have wood, metal walls or a dome.
With mud packed between the logs,
It's still the same.
With mud floors and a kind loving heart,
It's no game.
Why should it matter whether we're rich or poor?
We all must come through the same door.
Some have money, fine clothes and new cars.
They are still counted as just a human star.
I have lived in a dog house, cracks filled with mud.
I am no different than you.
We are all one with the same blood.
Some people think they are better and have more class.
Everyone can see they are just on the other side of the glass.
Rich or poor, bound or free, how much different can you be.
You can be beautiful, ugly, tall or small,
Or maybe can't see,
We were born in this world a baby all the same.
We all have dreams, some very wild and some tame.
With all you prestige, money, power and better things,
You are no different, you are still the same.

(132)
We are all numbered,
As the desert of sand.
You came into this world naked,
The same as any other man.

Anna Huffman & Family

Begin Manhood

Now that manhood has begun,
>Sing a song you have never sung.

Of things gone past.
>That could never last.

Now dreams built upon dreams,
>That could make the past dreams scream.

Now I will write upon the slate,
>These dreams will never be too late.

I'll live one day at a time,
>And spin around, as upon a dime.

And sing the songs of tomorrow,
>As the past has many sorrows.

There's a new tomorrow beginning,
>And the old life ending.

Many hopes and wishes pending.
>I'll build my dreams on solid ground,

And weigh each dream I have found.
>There have been sad and lonely years.

I must conquer without fear.
>I'll wipe my slate clean,

And watch the sparkles gleam.
>Who said I wouldn't reach my goal.

It may not be riches in silver and gold,
    I'll always look forward with outreached hands.
Across the years and pray for a long life span.
    As I weigh the past,
It wasn't meant to last.
    Now I weigh the future to be.
I thank God I have been set free,
    To make of life a fine hombre.
Making out of life what I want to be.
    The finest of man, and working bee.
To have and to hold,
    A good loving heart and soul.

Bernice Mongro

Boy To Man

Now that my guardianship for you is ended,
I can't cross this last forbidden span.
But love and tears and prayers together blended,
To guide your steps from boyhood to man.

You walk alone with God from this day forward,
To make of life whatsoever be His will,
Provided you surrender to His guidance,
Allowing love of God in hour heart to fill.

I cherish all our days far beyond the sun.
The happy days that blot out every other.
I bow my head to thank God you were born, son.
And oh, I'm so proud to be your Mother.

Anna Huffman & Family

Ruth Oldham

Ruth Oldham is 62 years old and was born in Mansfield, Ohio.

She likes swimming and reading magazines.

Anna Huffman & Family

When Tomorrow Starts Without Me

When tomorrow starts without me,

And I'm not there to see.

If the sun should rise and find your eyes,

All filled with tears for me,

I wish so much you wouldn't cry,

The way you did today,

While thinking of many things,

We didn't get to say.

I know how much you love,

As much as I love you,

And each time that you think of me,

I know you'll miss me too.

If tomorrow starts without me,

Please try to understand,

That an angel came and called my name,

And took me by the hand,

And said my place was ready,

In Heaven far above,

And that I would have to leave behind,

All those I dearly love.

But as I turned to walk away,
A tear fell from my eye,
For all my life I'd always thought,
I didn't want to die.
I had so much to live for,
So much yet to do.
It seemed almost impossible that I was leaving you.

I though of all the yesterdays.
The good ones and the bad.
I thought of all the love we shared,
All the fun we had.

So when tomorrow starts without me,
Don't think we are far apart.
For every time you think of me,
I'm right here in your heart.

                                          In loving memory of my
                                          husband, Ron Oldham.
                                          Passed April 2, 2003

                                                                       Ruth Oldham

To Whom It Concerns

Don't take anything for granted.

You might think your health is good,

Until something goes wrong,

And you lose someone you love.

Your health may start to decline,

When you worry about bills,

And the stress takes over.

Things are not the same as they used to be.

You find that you can't do the things you used to do.

The way the world is going today,

Everybody needs to slow down,

And stop and smell the roses.

Ruth Oldham

Anna Huffman & Family

Danyell Robernette

I was born and raised in Catawba County, North Carolina. Living here all my life.

I'm 29 years old and have 2 girls, whom I love very much.

I like reading books.

I've been married for 3 years.

Anna Huffman & Family

US

**THINGS AREN'T ALWAYS PERFECT,
IT'S TRUE I KNOW.
BUT MY LOVE FOR YOU,
ONLY GROWS.
NO MATTER HOW OFTEN WE FIGHT,
WE'RE NEVER MAD,
AS WE TURN OUT THE LIGHTS.
IT IS YOU THAT I THINK OF EACH DAY,
BECAUSE I LOVE YOU MORE,
THAN WORDS CAN SAY.**

Danyell Robernette

Hope

They all said that it wouldn't last,
> But my heart said that I had to give it my best.

So, I closed my eyes and held on tight,
> Hoping that my heart is right.

Danyell Robernette

Risk

(Dedicated to all who are in need of help)

To laugh is to risk appearing a fool.

To weep is to risk appearing sentimental.

To reach out for another is to risk involvement.

To expose feelings is to risk rejection.

To place you dreams before the crowd is to risk ridicule.

To love is to risk not being loved in return.

To go forward in the face of overwhelming odds is to risk failure.

But risks must be taken, because the greatest hazard in life is to risk nothing.

The person who risks nothing does nothing,

Has nothing,

Is nothing.

He may avoid suffering and sorrow,

But he cannot learn, feel, change, grow, or love.

Chained by his certitude's, he is a slave.

He has forfeited his freedom.

Only a person who takes risks is free

Anonymous

Christmas In Heaven

(Our family dedicates this poem to all families, large and small)

I see the countless Christmas trees around the world below,
With tiny lights, like Heaven's stars reflecting on the snow.
The sight is so spectacular, please wipe away the tear.
For I am spending Christmas with Jesus Christ this year.
I hear the many Christmas songs that people hold so dear,
But the sounds of music can't compare with the Christmas Choir up here.
I have no words to tell you, the joy their voices bring,
For it is beyond description, to hear the angels sing.
I know how much you miss me, I see the pain inside your heart,
But I am not so far away, we really aren't apart.
So be happy for me dear ones, you know I hold you dear.
And be glad I'm spending Christmas with Jesus Christ this year.
I sent you each a special gift, from my heavenly home above,
I sent you each a memory of my undying love.
After all, love is a gift more precious than pure gold,
It was always most important in the stories Jesus told.
Please love and keep each other; as my Father said to do,
For I can't count the blessing or love he has for each of you.
So have a Merry Christmas and wipe away that tear;
Remember, I am spending Christmas with Jesus Christ this year.

Unknown

My Family-Poems & Poetry From The Heart-The Way We Were

Anna Huffman & Family

My Family-Poems & Poetry From The Heart-The Way We Were

Anna Huffman & Family

www.ingramcontent.com/pod-product-compliance
Lightning Source LLC
Chambersburg PA
CBHW031959080426
42735CB00007B/451